Olivia has a bad cough. Her father gives her cough **medicine.**

Olivia's medicine is an **over-the-counter drug.** It will help stop Olivia's cough.

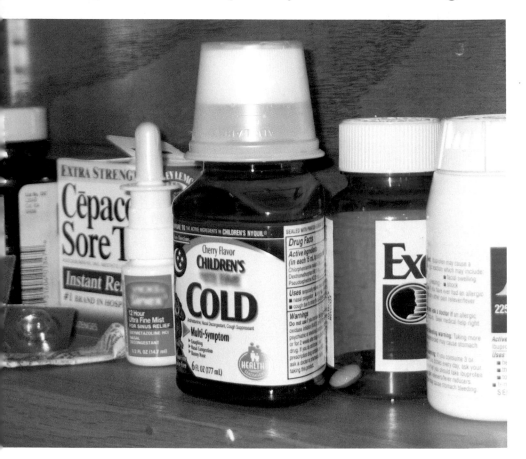

Her father buys it at the store. What over-the-counter drugs can you find at the store?

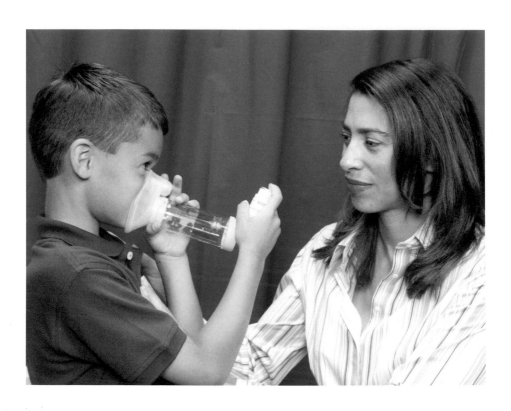

Alex has **asthma**. His mother gives him asthma medicine. Alex's medicine is a **prescription** drug. It will help Alex when he has trouble breathing.

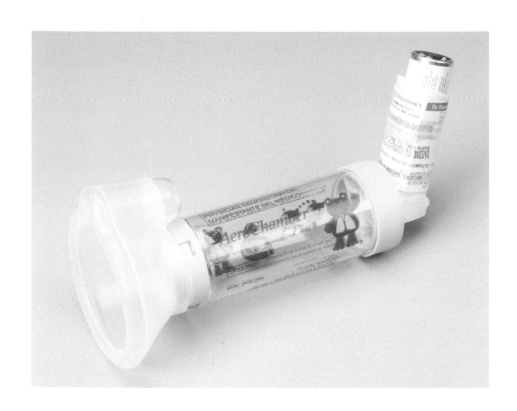

Alex's doctor orders the drug for him.
The medicine is only for Alex. His
mother buys it at the prescription
counter at the store.

Olivia and Alex only take medicine their parents or doctors give them. Their parents read and follow the directions.

The right amount of medicine can help them get well. The wrong amount or the wrong medicine could hurt them!

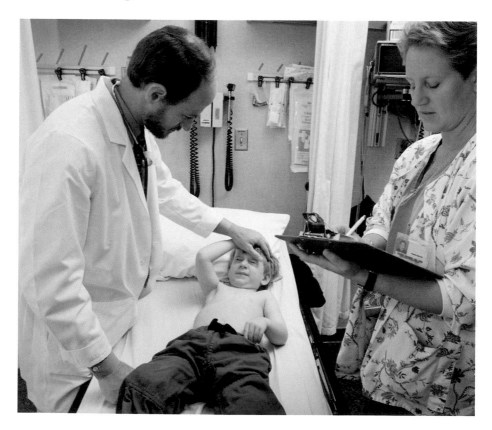

Medicines and vitamins are drugs. Drugs change the way your body works.

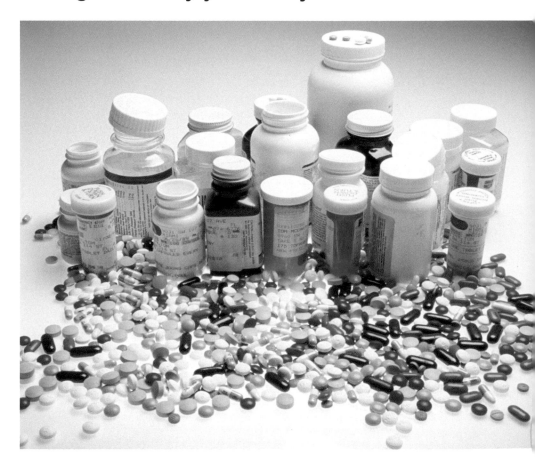

Some drugs help you stay healthy. Others
help you when you are sick. These
drugs are called **medicinal drugs.**

Some drugs won't help you stay healthy. They may even hurt your body or make you sick. These drugs are called **non-medicinal drugs.**

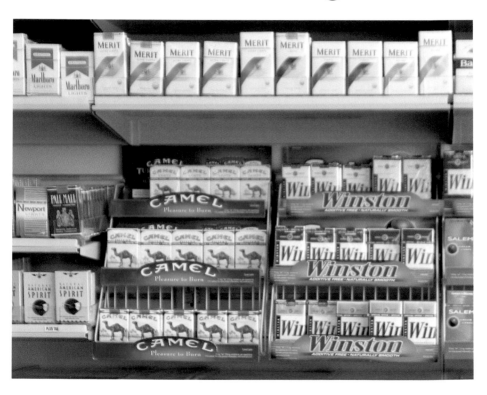

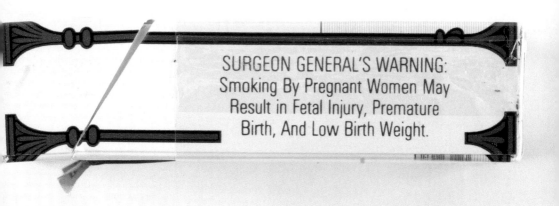

SURGEON GENERAL'S WARNING:
Smoking By Pregnant Women May
Result in Fetal Injury, Premature
Birth, And Low Birth Weight.

Alcohol and **nicotine** are non-medicinal drugs. They can be harmful to the body. They may cause illness and even death.

Some people **misuse** these or other drugs. They might take drugs when they are sad, lonely, or bored.

They hope the drugs will change the way they feel. But often the drugs make them very sick. Sometimes people can't stop using drugs!

Tommy's grandma smokes cigarettes.
Most days, she coughs a lot. She also
has trouble breathing.

Tommy wonders why she smokes. Do you know why?

17

Cigarettes have **tobacco.** Tobacco has nicotine. It makes it hard for people to stop smoking.

Tobacco can
cause lung
cancer and
other illnesses.

19

At parties, Sue's aunt always has a drink in her hand. She talks loudly and acts silly. Sometimes she falls down.

Why do you
think Sue's aunt
acts this way?

Her aunt drinks too much alcohol. Drinks like beer and wine have alcohol. Alcohol changes how people feel and act.

Drinking too much alcohol makes some people feel sad. It can make others feel angry. Over time, too much alcohol can hurt the body and mind.

Most adults can drink some alcohol and stop. Others, like Sue's aunt, can't stop. They need help!

People who drink alcohol and drive can hurt or kill themselves and others. Drinking and driving is against the law.

It's everyone's job to be smart about drugs. Olivia and Alex take only the drugs their parents and doctors give to them.

Olivia and Alex stay away from non-medicinal drugs. You can too!

What I've Learned

- Only take medicine your parents, a trusted adult, or doctor gives you.

- The wrong medicine or wrong amount of medicine can hurt you.

- Some drugs are not medicine. They do not help you stay healthy. Nicotine and alcohol are these kinds of drugs.

- Nicotine makes it hard to stop smoking.

- Alcohol can make people feel and act differently. Alcohol makes it hard for some people to stop drinking it.

- Some people misuse drugs when they feel bad. Sometimes they can't stop using drugs.

- Drinking and driving is against the law.

Have a Drug-Free Plan

A friend may ask you to try drugs. Learn how to say no.
Practice these lines with someone.

Person 1: Want to smoke?
Person 2: No, way! I like breathing.

Person 1: Try this drug. It will make you feel great.
Person 2: I like the way I feel. Drugs only make you feel
sick!

Person 1: Come on. Have a drink. It'll make you do silly
things.
Person 2: No, thanks! I like being myself.

Person 1: Try this drug. Everybody's doing it!
Person 2: No, not everyone's doing it—because I'm NOT
doing it.

Person 1: If you were my friend, you'd do this drug
with me.
Person 2: If you keep doing drugs, I can't be your friend!

Books and Websites

Books

Bryant-Mole, Karen. *Talking about Drugs.* Austin, TX: Raintree Steck-Vaughn Publishers, 2000.

MacGregor, Cynthia. *Refuse to Use.* New York: Rosen Publishing Group, 2003.

Murphy, Patricia J. *Staying Happy.* Lerner Publications Company, 2006.

Westcott, Patsy. *Why Do People Take Drugs?* Austin, TX: Raintree Steck-Vaughn Publishers, 2001.

Websites

KidsHealth
http://www.kidshealth.org/kids

Resources for Parents and Teachers, American Council for Drug Education
http://www.acde.org/youth

Can We Talk?
http://www.canwetalk.org

National Institute on Drug Abuse, National Institute of Health
http://www.nida.nih.gov

Glossary

alcohol: a liquid found in drinks like wine or beer

asthma: a condition that can cause trouble breathing

medicinal drugs: drugs that can keep the body healthy or treat illness

medicine: a drug used to treat an illness

misuse: to use something the wrong way

nicotine: a drug found in tobacco and in cigarettes, chaw, and cigars

non-medicinal drugs: drugs that affect the body but that do not treat an illness

over-the-counter drug: a drug that can be bought without a doctor's order

prescription: a doctor's order for a drug

tobacco: leaves of the tobacco plant used for smoking or chewing

Index

alcohol, 13, 22–25, 28

drinking and driving, 25, 28

medicine, 3, 6–11, 28
misusing drugs, 14–15, 22, 28

nicotine, 13, 18, 28
non-medicinal drugs, 12–13, 27

over-the-counter drugs, 4, 5

prescription drugs, 6, 7
proper use of medicine, 8–9, 26, 28

saying no to drugs, 26, 29
smoking, 16–18

tobacco, 18, 19, 28

Photo Acknowledgments

The photographs in this book appear courtesy of: © Todd Strand/Independent Picture Service, front cover, pp. 3, 4, 6, 7, 8, 13, 16, 17, 18, 20, 21, 22, 23, 26, 27; © Sam Lund/Independent Picture Service, p. 5; © Royalty-Free/ CORBIS, pp. 9, 11, 14; PhotoDisc Royalty Free by Getty Images, pp. 10, 15, 19, 24, 25; © Rick Friedman/ CORBIS, p. 12.